CHASE ROWICK

HIGH PERFORMANCE HABITS

**The Ultimate Guide to Developing Good
Habits, Learn the Successful Techniques on
How to Develop Good Habits For Life**

Descrierea CIP a Bibliotecii Naţionale a României
CHASE ROWICK
   HIGH PERFORMANCE HABITS. The Ultimate Guide to Developing Good Habits, Learn the Successful Techniques on How to Develop Good Habits For Life / Chase Rowick – Bucharest: Editura My Ebook, 2021
   ISBN

CHASE ROWICK

HIGH PERFORMANCE HABITS
The Ultimate Guide to Developing Good Habits, Learn the Successful Techniques on How to Develop Good Habits For Life

My Ebook Publishing House
Bucharest, 2021

TABLE OF CONTENTS

INTRODUCTION

"Prevention is better than cure" – This is a famous and apt proverb for bad habits. Thus, it is always better to prevent them rather than get started and quit later. Do you have a bad habit you want to change? Then, you should make the best move now!

Bad habits can control your life. They can transform you into someone you don't want to be. Depending on your choice, you may want to stop eating unhealthy foods, want to quit smoking, turn around negative thoughts and a lot more.

Whether you wish to remove a bad habit or desire to practice a healthy or good habit, you don't need to worry about it. There are various ways to solve your major concerns.

Some people claim that changing a habit is a tremendous struggle. They usually spend several months or even years just to change their bad habits. But, some of them fail. Are you one of them? If yes, then you have to read this eBook now!

This guide allows you to understand how to create good habits. So, continue reading and be ready for a big change!

CHAPTER 1

BAD HABIT BASICS

If you want things to be different in your life, then there is no point in doing things over and over again. If you do, you will surely get the same results.

To get a different result, you have to try a different approach. Thus, you need to move from your comfort zone.

Don't know where to begin with? Then, you need to understand first everything about bad habit formation.

Bad Habit Formation

Habit formation is the process by which behaving a certain way becomes automatic. If you impulsively reach for a cigarette the moment you wake up in the morning, then that's a habit.

Old habits are difficult to break and new habits are too hard to form. This statement is really true because the behavioural patterns you repeat most often are literally etched into your neural pathways.

Furthermore, habits serve as a mechanism for rapid problem solving. Whenever you encounter pain, your brain instantly searches for a way to prevent it. Likewise, whenever you encounter gratification, your brain stores those neurological connections to gain from that satisfaction in the future. In some cases, people use alcohol and foods as a mechanism to get out of boredom and depression.

The habits that are closely related to your mechanisms for feeling pleasure and out of pain are usually the toughest to remove because these habits are hard to change.

At present, more and more people are trapped in some bad habits that they wish they never had. To change, you need to have a high motivation and intention. Experts claim that it is easy to develop bad habits, especially when a person is young. But, you have to bear in mind that a bad habit is a process that begins from your mind. Thus, you can remove it if you really want to.

Types of Habits

Habits have two distinct types and here they are:

1. *Behavioural Habits* – Chewing hair, nail biting, cracking knuckles are the common examples of bad behavioural habits. These habits are annoying personally, or to other people. These are best removed by altering your activity altogether or changing the bad one for a good one.

2. *Addictive Habits* – Liquor, smoking and drugs have a hold on the physical body, causing some uncomfortable feelings when the activity is stopped.

How Does Someone Develop a Bad Habit?

Some people are clueless when it comes to different causes of bad habits. If you are one of them, you should start expanding your ideas. For additional help, here are the reasons why some people develop a bad habit:

> ➢ *Engage in Any Specific Behaviour* – Habits are behaviours that happen automatically, habitually and subconsciously. When engaging in a particular

behaviour with favourable outcomes, people tend to repeat that behaviour.

> ***Reap the Rewards*** - Whether it is a bad or good habit, it can be a matter of opinion. Say for instance, smoking is considered as a bad habit. But, some people say that that smoking calms them down and that pushes them to smoke cigarettes every day.

> ***Do It Again*** – Habit formation depends on reinforcement. Some people tend to do things that will lead to negative or positive reinforcement. Negative reinforcement is the removal of an unfavourable situation while positive reinforcement is the presentation of a favourable outcome.

> ***Do It Again and Again*** – Even if bad habits can result in bad consequences, the quick gratification is what allows them to be kept. However, these habits will have to get done eventually and they will become more difficult tasks.

Though it is hard to get rid of bad habits, you don't need to worry about it. You just have to know what you need to do and where to begin.

CHAPTER 2

KNOW WHAT YOU WANT TO CHANGE
AND MAKE A LIST OF THE BENEFITS

Bad habits come in multiple forms, from small ones that just irritate others to serious ones that are extremely dangerous to health. Getting rid of bad habits is possible, but it is not too easy.

To stay away from your bad habits, you have to do the first step – KNOW WHAT YOU WANT TO CHANGE. That's very simple, right? But, changing your routine just to get rid of your bad habits is really a daunting task.

Top Bad Habits You Want to Change

Most people desire to get rid of their bad habits. But, they can't easily do it because they don't know where to begin. Here are some of the different habits you want to change:

Behavioural/Annoying Bad Habits

➢ Interrupting others

➢ Eating with your mouth open

➢ Picking your teeth in public

➢ Snapping at people in anger

➢ Shouting

➢ Laziness

Addictive/Dangerous Habits

➢ Drinking too much alcohol

➢ Smoking

➢ Overeating and a lot more

Get rid of your bad habits or you hurt others, run the risk of losing friends and ruining your health – what will you pick? Like others, you will surely want to control your bad habits.

Why do You Need to List Down Your Bad Habits?

Listing down your bad habits is the best way to know what you want to change. Through the use of your journal, you are guaranteed that you will never forget something.

Here are the top reasons why you need to know what you want to change and why you have to make a list of its benefits:

➢ Know how many bad habits you opt to change

➢ Easily recognize why you need to get rid of your bad habits

➢ Understand its implications in your daily life

➢ Easily make plans on how to remove your bad habits

Say for instance, if you keep on picking your teeth or eating with your mouth open, your friends may refrain you from inviting you out again. In addition, interrupting or snapping at others will cause arguments that can affect your social life. If you keep on smoking or drinking, your body will surely become weak and that leads to various health issues and even early death.

How to Stick with Your List?

Upon listing down all the bad habits you want to change, you are on your way to motivate yourself to stick with your list. How can you do it? The answers are very simple and here they are:

➢ *Focus on its Benefits* – If you find it hard to stick with your list, you simply focus on the benefits you will get after overcoming your bad habits. Through this, you will be more enticed to pursue what you have started.

➢ *Know Your Limitations* – At first, you can't totally get rid of your bad habits. As advised, your first goal is to minimize your bad habits. Say for instance, if you puff cigarettes several times a day, you have to limit it until you successfully remove it.

➢ *Don't Make Excuses* – If you really want to change your bad habits, you have to do everything to improve your daily activities. Thus, you should refrain from giving shallow excuses just to continue your habits.

These basic steps are easy to follow. So, make a right move now and start listing down the bad habits you want to change!

CHAPTER 3

BE COMMITTED TO CHANGE

Overcoming your bad habits or achieving even the simplest objectives in your life requires you to learn the meaning of COMMITMENT. Without commitment, you can't achieve anything.

Whether it is your vices or about your work, everything you ever achieved sprouted from a commitment you made. Thus, learning how to commit is not merely about making commitments; it is also about keeping those promises in the face of unforeseen or foreseen hurdles.

Tips on How to Commit Right and Change Your Bad Habits

There are several ways you can stay committed and change your bad habits. If you don't know what to do, simply use the following tips as your guide:

➤ ***Don't Be Involved, Stay Committed*** – If you want to get rid of your bad habits, you have to spend enough time and effort to make it possible. Being involved means you are not committed enough and if you are not committed enough, that thing you have been working on will never be realized.

➤ ***If You Will Not Learn How to Commit, Someone Else Will*** - Remember that you are living in a highly competitive environment. Unlike others, you have to learn not to fight. Just like you, there are thousands of people who opt to change their bad habits and to live a better life. If you just sit back, relax and do nothing, expect that you will never reach your goal.

➤ ***Never Give Up*** - Take note that quitting is also a lesson. You always pay for that lesson with the time you lost. But, sometimes you find yourself with your back to the wall and you have to take radical measures to save the day.

➤ *Free Your Mind* – If you free your mind, the rest will follow. Once you are committed to something, there are no more choices to be made but to focus on your goal.

A true commitment to personal change requires three major things and here they are:

1. *Vision* – It is great if you know exactly what you would like the NEW YOU to be like. However, it is not always necessary. All you need is to be open to imagining yourself in the future.

2. *Promise* – When you commit to change, you unreservedly make a promise. This promise is not to your sister, brother, husband or any members of the family. The promise you make is to YOURSELF. It is like writing a check with your mind. The best way you cash that check depends on your actions.

3. *Work* - If you are moving with purpose, your work will be great. Work means spending your energy at something that may change you. Commitment is a

perfect ingredient for change. When you commit with your promise, vision and work, it pays off in something better.

Are you ready to commit and start changing your bad habits? Then, don't just make a list of the things you want to change. You have to focus and begin immediate action to reach your goals.

CHAPTER 4

REWARD YOURSELF

Getting rid of your bad habits is not as easy as you think. It involves a lot of time and effort. Since it cannot be done in just a single click of your finger, you have to stay focused.

If you already removed your bad habits, Congratulations! You are now one step closer to beginning good habits and healthy living.

Just like others who already removed their bad habits, you have to do yourself a favor – REWARD YOURSELF.

Rewarding yourself is rejuvenating and inspiring. To reward yourself, you have to make rewards meaningful. The first rule of rewards is that they should make you feel good and should have value. Your reward should also be immediate. In short, when you achieve a determined goal, either big or small, you get the reward that matches.

There are two types of rewards and here they are:

> *Extrinsic* – Coming from the outside like going to a spa, buying a CD, getting praise from others and a lot more.

> *Intrinsic* – The reward is in how the action makes you feel like content, proud or victorious.

Even if rewards that change your inner life are more significant in the long run, extrinsic rewards serve as indispensable pats-on-the-back on the road to change.

Tips for Rewards

If you opt to reward yourself after overcoming your bad habits, you need to consider the following tips:

> Always reward the positives but never punish slip-ups

> When rewarding yourself, get to know what you really value. You may be motivated by different things like praise, beauty and money.

> Celebrate small accomplishments

> Inform others about your success

- Don't over-reward. If someone raves about a mediocre accomplishment, you feel manipulated and patronized. Make the reward match the output or effort

- Celebrate with others, particularly mentors

- Create a written and signed contract with yourself which you track the behavioural changes and rewards

- Re-examine your goals and rewards. If they don't work, don't hesitate to change them

With these various tips, you can easily reward yourself in a more positive and effective way.

Ways to Reward Yourself

Rewarding yourself is not a tough task. There are various options to choose from and here are some of them:

- Compliment yourself

- Create an actual trophy

- Give yourself badges of honor for distinct levels of accomplishment

- Take a vacation along with your friends

- Take a day off from any goal activities

- Watch your all-time favorite movies

- Go for a spa treatment or massage

- Purchase yourself a gift certificate

- Find some time to be by yourself

- Buy something you want and a lot more!

Rewarding yourself is a great way to keep motivation for changing your bad habits. Your desired rewards, however, shouldn't come in any form that affects your good habits.

If you find it hard to come up with ideas for goals and suitable rewards, don't hesitate to work with your trainer to set up a milestone system. You also need to think small rewards for mini-goals and big rewards for attaining the long-term goals.

CHAPTER 5

START SLOW AND GO FOR CONSISTENCY

Effective goal-setting helps you achieve what you desire. It can also have a significant effect on the way you feel about yourself. Whether you want to get rid of simple or dangerous bad habits, you have to start slow and go for consistency. The main question is, how can you do this?

How to Start Slow

If you don't know where to begin, here are the steps you need to follow to start slow:

Step 1: **Focus on Small Goals** – If you have lots of bad habits you want to change, you have to focus first on small goals. You don't need to be in a hurry. Just be firm with your plans and prepare for a new challenge in your life.

Step 2: **Don't Pressure Yourself** – Though you are eager to remove your bad habits, you don't need to pressure yourself. Just stick with your plan and do the best you can every day.

Step 3: **Always Remember Your Promises** – If you are eager to get rid of your bad habits, you have to make sure that you are fully committed with your decisions. When you start to change your bad habits, you have to pursue it, whatever it takes.

Step 4: **Stay Away from Temptations** - To remove your bad habits, you need to stay away from temptations. Say for instance, you want to stop drinking too much alcohol, the best thing that you can do is not to store any brand of alcohol in your freezer. You also stay away from your friends who keep on tempting you to drink more alcohol.

Step 5: **Remind Yourself of the Benefits** – If you find it hard to get rid of your bad habits, simply remind yourself about the different benefits you will receive after overcoming those bad habits. Through this, you will be more encouraged to stick with your plan.

At first, changing your bad habits may be too tough. But, as time passes by, you will surely find it fast and easy.

How to Go for Consistency

Consistency is one of those vague qualities that everyone desires. If you want to go for consistency, you have to consider the following:

Change the Way You Think

To change the way you think, you have to be realistic. Take note that you won't be completely consistent in an instant.

As advised, you are not going to be consistent 100% of the time. Remember, you are just a human. It is okay to make mistakes and rarely getting lax about your unswerving habit is understandable.

In addition, you also need to build your self-control. You cannot have consistency without developing your willpower. To build your will power you will have to practice every day. Say for instance, if you want to be consistent about eating in a healthy way, always ensure that you have healthy options.

It is also best to make sure that your actions are always matched with your words. If you are consistent, you don't have say one thing and do something else. You cannot be inconsistent in your behavior and expect yourself to behave consistently in other parts of your life.

Similar with others, you also need to eliminate negative thinking. This is the bane of consistency and of willpower. If you think negatively, you are making yourself likely seize to your consistent actions.

Building Your Consistency

Consistency is great, but being consistent is too easy if you set specific goals. These goals will assist you to behave consistently and offer you something to strive for. Depending on your choices, you can see a variety of goals in different areas of your life.

Take note that if you try and do everything at once, you will overwhelm yourself. As a result, it will make it a lot harder for you to be consistent. So, make gradual changes instead of jumping in head first.

When building your consistency, it is best to set specific boundaries. These boundaries will make it easier to be consistent. Setting a boundary means setting constraints on exactly when and how you are going to do certain things.

Maintaining Consistency

If you don't stay motivated, you will never change your bad habits. You will fall back into old patterns of behavior instead of sticking with the new patterns you are trying to make.

CHAPTER

GET SUPPORT

Do you want to get rid of your bad habits? There are various ways to do it. Instead of thinking about what you need to do, why not get support from experts?

Getting support from experts is fast and easy. You just have to find the right person, things or other sources to answer your needs.

Multiple Options to Get Support

Changing your bad habits may seem too tough, especially when you are not fully aware of the different things you need to do. For your guide, here are the different options you may consider:

- **Books** – This is one of the best sources you can use to get enough clues on how to break your bad habits. Depending on your choice, you can get books related to creating a good habit, developing a healthy activity and a lot more.

- **Family Members** – Your family is always there to help you. With their countless tips and reminders, you will soon realize that you are getting rid of your bad habits. Just make sure that you follow the tips suggested by your parents or relatives.

- **Doctors** – There are various specialists that focus on the behavioral patterns of an individual. If you wish to get their help to get rid of your bad habits, make sure that you are selecting the best and reliable one.

Since there are various options to choose from, you are sure to be easily able to get rid of your bad habits. So, don't just sit back and relax. Make the right move and explore more on how to solve your major concerns.

Benefits of Asking Support from Others

If you are young, you may find it hard to remove your bad habits. Through asking support from others, you will get the following benefits:

- ❑ Able to know what you need to do to break your bad habits

- ❑ Know how to recognize things or situations that can trigger your bad habits to develop

- ❑ Understand the different ways to overcome your bad habits

- ❑ Able to experience a healthy and active life

As you can see, there are various benefits you can get after asking for support from reliable sources. So, the choice is yours! If you are ready to change your bad habits, this is your chance to make the right decision.

Upon overcoming your bad habits, you are on your way to a dynamic and better life.

CHAPTER 7

STAY MOTIVATED

Even if it seems that everything is negative around you, you need to stay motivated in order for you to achieve your goals and hopes in life. You cannot control what happens in your life but you can control how you will take action to change these things. Turn the negative into a positive atmosphere and begin to be more motivated in achieving your ultimate goals.

Be Guided to Keep You Motivated

If you have attitude for anticipation, you will likely have what you anticipate. You only need to expect that something great will happen and it will happen for you. You must focus on the things that you can control rather than those which you cannot. Do not worry on the things that are beyond your control and don't allow yourself to be stuck in something that prevents you from developing. The sooner you can get rid of unnecessary things, the faster you can move on to the next level.

Embrace that positive information and fill your mind with things that will inspire and motivate you. Reading a good book that talks about a nice topic will ignite motivation in you. In fact, you need to keep reminders that will tell how capable you are in achieving things. Perhaps, you need to be with optimistic people and talk about topics that can be productive and motivating for you.

Do you know that words can be a creative force? Say to yourself what you want to happen. Make an affirmation in writing and paste it on a spot where you can refer to it every single day so that you are well reminded and motivated of what you actually want. Instead of making the same mistakes all over again, learn from them and move on. Yes, it is a known fact that we are not perfect and we always have the chance to commit mistakes but the thing is, we should learn from each mistake.

Plan for Success

If you have time, try to make a plan to allow yourself to think of better ideas for improving your productivity and getting results. Your motivation in accomplishing your desires can be greatly followed through a definitive plan that you made. When you successfully achieve your goals, celebrate it whether it's small or big. When you try to reward yourself, you keep yourself motivated too.

Most of the time, we simply forget how much we have achieved in our life. On this note, you may refer to your achievements during times when you need to be reminded that you are simply a winner. These victories will help you stay motivated and keep achieving goals to the next level. Day by day, you should be inspired by the accomplishments that you have made in your previous endeavours, that's the only way you stay motivated.

A positive attitude can be contagious; the mind that is filled with positive thoughts will produce more positive outcomes. Get more opportunities and turn them into victories. Signify your life with proper motivation so that you will reach all your aspirations in life according to your plan. Achieving every set goal, you must think, believe and speak to achieve it. Staying motivated is the top priority to realize your dreams. Remember, a positive perspective is always a contributing factor to stay motivated and accomplish goals.

Staying motivated is the only way to achieve things in life. Focus, determination, and passion are contributing factors to keep yourself motivated and get the outcome that you want. When you focus yourself, there is a big chance that you will accomplish everything that you have decided to attain.

CHAPTER 8

BELIEVE IN YOU

Believing in yourself can sometimes be hard, especially when you feel unworthy and unloved. When the truth is, you are capable and worthy. Don't let negative thoughts eat you and hinder you from achieving what you truly want in life. There is so much that life has to offer, be ready to embrace all of it.

Recognizing your skills and the numerous good things about you will significantly help you to believe in yourself. Think of the things that people compliment you about. Look at those things that you can do well and feel more comfortable in doing them and other things also. You need to set your goals and make way to achieve them. Expose yourself outside and discover a lot of things that you can actually do.

See failures as learning and take your shortcomings as motivation to be better. The first thing you do when you believe in yourself is trying even if you think you can't do it at first. The wrong belief that we often stick to is that, we are afraid to be wrong so we end up not trying. This negative mindset will only put you passively. The thing is, you should try new things so that you will learn how to handle them by your own.

Also, you may talk to people who love you and find a better perception on yourself. Sometimes, we are reluctant to see the good things in ourselves but others will remind us how good we are. When you are simply poisoned by the things around you, you may take some rest and get prepared for the next battle. Things around you can be overwhelming; taking a break would just be the right thing to do.

Guidelines to Believe

If you believe in something, do it. If you think that something important needs to be done, then don't ever hesitate to do it. You also need to get realistic expectations and think that things will fall into place just the way you want it to be. You need to balance your thinking about things that may go right and wrong. Making mistakes is done by everyone, it is inevitable. Recognize yourself in other people and realize that we are all worthwhile. If they can do better things, you can do better things too.

One very important thing to believe in you is to stop degrading yourself. You have to stop underestimating your own capabilities. Do yourself a favor and never mind those negative things that other people say about you.

When you think of the positive things that you have, you can be able to achieve what you want in life.

When you focus yourself and move forward, you are simply letting go of the past which may not be helpful for you. Think about how to perform well in the future instead of burying yourself in the past. Rather, think of things like how you can't change that past and have a brighter future instead. If you have built confidence in yourself, you have a great probability that you can accomplish the things that you have planned to achieve.

The ultimate thing to believe in you is to love yourself and be who you really are. Don't ever dare to become someone who you aren't. If you truly know yourself, you will be successful in being the person you want to be. You should know that every person is unique in their own little way. Loving yourself means improving yourself to become better. When you do things by believing in yourself, you will be happy with the results.

BELIEVE IN YOU - three simple things that each individual have to be aware of. When things seem to fall apart, only you can make a difference. It is only you who can make a better change for your own self. This is an important factor in order to have a purposeful life and attain things you actually think you can't.

After reading this guide, you are now fully aware of the different things that you need to do to get what you really want. Whether you want to get rid of your bad habits or opt to create a good habit, you don't have to worry about. Anything you want can be easily achieved. It is simply a matter on how you make your own moves and decisions.

What are you waiting for? Start changing your daily routine. With this guide, you are on your way to your desired goal!

Printed by Libri Plureos GmbH in Hamburg,
Germany